ORDINARY PEOPLE CHANGE — THE — WORLD

I am Malala Yousafzai

BRAD MELTZER

illustrated by Christopher Eliopoulos

DIAL BOOKS FOR YOUNG READERS

I am **MALALA YOUSAFZAI.**

Let me tell you a few interesting things about myself.
I'm double-jointed and can bend my fingers all the way back.
I'm also really good at arm-wrestling my brothers.

I like cupcakes, but don't like candy. And I hate green peppers and eggplant, but love pizza.

Also, my favorite color is pink, and I love styling my hair.

I'm a Pashtun, part of a tribe of people from Afghanistan and Pakistan.

I'm Muslim, which means Islam is my religion, and I'm committed to peace and helping others.

Growing up, I lived in the Swat Valley, in northwest Pakistan.

IT MAY LOOK DIFFERENT HERE, BUT WE PLAY MANY OF THE SAME GAMES AS YOU, LIKE TAG AND HOPSCOTCH.

Girls are treated very differently from boys here.
If you're a girl, you're expected to get married, and walk
a few paces behind your husband to show he's in charge.
Also, you're expected to cover yourself when you're
outside your house.

Some women, like my mom, wear a scarf, called a niqab,
on their face. Others wear black robes, called burqas, that cover everything.
In my culture, that's the tradition.
To me, it seemed uncomfortable and unfair for someone to require you
to dress a certain way.

In fact, if you were a girl, you weren't even listed on the family tree.

It took more than that to improve things.
My mother was smart, funny, and strong—but because of the rules of our society, she was never taught to read.

My parents wanted me to soar.
I wanted that for myself too.

In local kite competitions,
some kites would fly high,
while others would plummet to the ground.
I felt like the plummeting kite.

My future would be cut down because I was a girl.

But my dad pushed back against these harsh rules with the most powerful tool of all: education.

He opened his own school, one of very few that girls could attend.

His school didn't have desks, or even bathrooms.
It was next to a smelly river.
But to me, it was paradise!
As a toddler, even before I could talk, I'd sit in classes with the older kids.

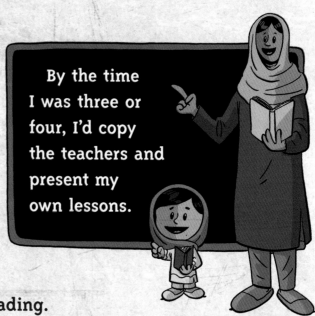

By five, I was reading.

But changing the world isn't easy.
One day, at the town garbage dump, I was throwing away our trash,
and I was worried about getting my nice shoes dirty.
Then I noticed something...

A girl.

She was covered in filth and flies,
sorting the trash into piles: paper, glass, bottle caps...

My father later told me that poor kids like her have to work in the dump, looking for things they can sell.

I kept picturing that girl with the dirty face.

That girl
could be me.

Or you.

That girl wasn't given an equal chance.
My father taught me that education was the best way
to empower people.
The world wouldn't be fair unless schooling was available
for everyone: boys and girls, rich and poor.

It might be hard to understand why school meant so much to me. But in a country where women had so few opportunities, we could explore through books.

At our school's public speaking competition, I wanted to win so badly—but my hands kept shaking. Everyone was watching. I kept losing my place.

H-HOLD ON... LET ME FIND MY SPOT.

I came in second place that day!
On top of that, it felt great to learn.

Not everyone was excited by my success.
When I was ten years old, a group called the Taliban took control of our valley.
They preferred the old traditions and believed that women should not
have any rights.

They were so against freedom for everyone, they told us to burn
our TVs and computers, as well as our CDs and DVDs.

Later, the Taliban left a letter on the school's gate.
They told my father if he didn't stop teaching girls,
bad things would happen.

They were threatening my father.
Now I was scared.

The Taliban treated us like little dolls they could control.
They wanted girls to be quiet.
Instead, my school fought back by holding a rally.

Later that year, the head of the Taliban announced that girls would no longer be allowed in school.

Only a few fought back.

Within days, my class of twenty-seven shrank to ten.

A friend of my father asked if any of the older girls would be willing to write about it for an international news organization called the BBC.

I was only eleven years old, but I asked my father...

I used a secret identity, the fake name Gul Makai, a heroine from an old Pashtun folktale.

My first entry was titled *I Am Afraid*.

From there...

Our story started to spread.

THIS GIRL IS AMAZING!

YOU GOTTA READ THIS...

TELEPHONE

I AM AFRAID

It traveled from Pakistan all the way around the world, people reading about how the Taliban was trying to stop letting girls get an education.

I AM AFRAID

I AM AFRAID

To get better at public speaking, I practiced my interviews in the mirror.

Soon, I was using my real name. And when the Taliban tried to close our school, I looked right into the camera and said:

THEY CANNOT STOP ME.

I WILL GET MY EDUCATION.

Eventually, the Taliban got what they wanted.
They closed our school—but I wouldn't let it stop me.
I started going to a secret school, hiding my books under my shawl.
Most important, I kept telling my story.
To other students...

To adults...

Even to politicians.

I'D LIKE TO PRESENT YOU WITH OUR FIRST NATIONAL YOUTH PEACE PRIZE.

THANK YOU.

NOW I'D LIKE TO PRESENT YOU WITH OUR REQUEST FOR A GIRLS' SCHOOL.

PRIME MINISTER OF PAKISTAN YOUSAF RAZA GILANI

This will sound scary, but by the time I was fourteen, the Taliban threatened to hurt me if I kept speaking out.
They didn't like the ideas I was putting into the world.
They didn't like that I had power.

My father told me: If you believe in something greater than yourself, your voice will multiply.
I didn't realize how right he was...

. . . or how quickly my world was about to change.
Eventually, my school reopened, and I was on the bus, coming home.
It was a normal day.

My only worry was about how I did on the exam I just took.

I remember some of the girls were singing.

Outside, I saw the road filled with life.

There was a boy selling ice cream.

I was happy.

The truth is, I don't remember the attack. My friends told me what happened later.

They told me a member of the Taliban climbed on board.

WHO IS MALALA?

I was the only girl whose face was not covered.

They told me his hand was shaking as he pulled the trigger.

And then . . .

Everything went black.

Five days later, I woke up in a hospital in England.
I had been badly hurt—shot in the face.
My left eye looked different now.
But the Taliban made a mistake.
They thought their bullets would silence me.
Instead...

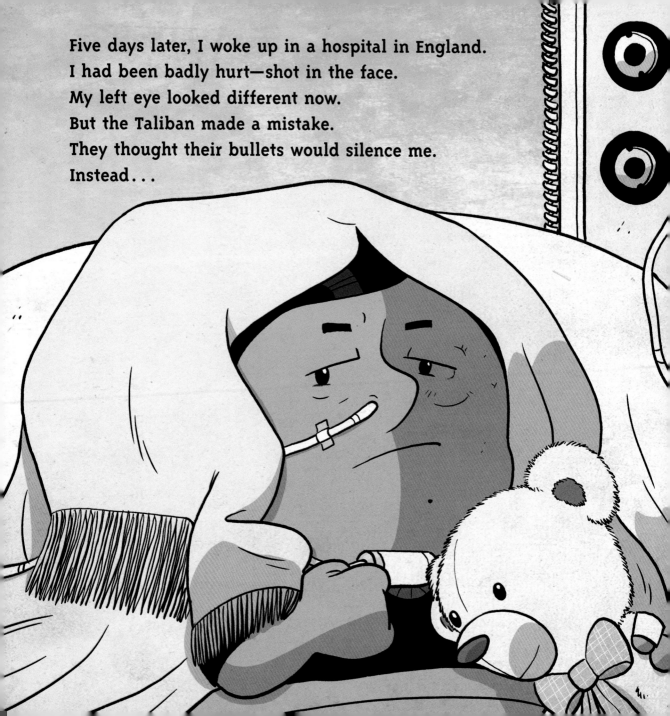

I had an even bigger chance to tell my story.
More people were suddenly paying attention.

Eventually, I learned to smile and wink again.
I started doing interviews for TV programs in other countries.

And meeting with more leaders who could create real change.

When I was younger, my family and I temporarily became refugees—
people who are forced from their home because of war.
I never forgot that.
So I also visited Syrian refugees who hadn't been in school for three years.

We created our own organization—Malala Fund—
to open schools for children all over the world.

In my life, people tried to silence me.
They didn't like that I was strong,
and outspoken, and the most powerful
thing of all: educated.
They saw me as a threat to their power.
And they were right.

I may be small, but I am mighty.
You are mighty too.
Education scares those who want to control us.
Our voices scare them.
Equality scares them.
But that's how we move the world forward.
Reading. Learning. Thinking. Speaking up.
These are gifts that are yours to use.

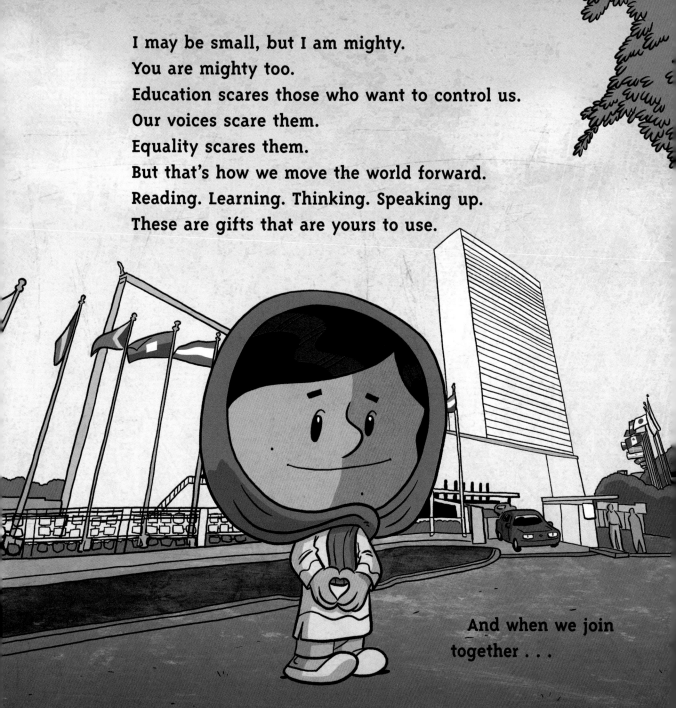

And when we join
together . . .

We are unstoppable.

I am an ordinary girl whose life was transformed by teachers and learning.
There are millions of others who need similar help.
That's why I will not be quiet.
The world doesn't change unless you speak up.
Use your voice. Help those who need it.

As I said at the United Nations:
"We must believe in the power and the strength of our words.
Our words can change the world...
Let us pick up our books and pens.
They are our most powerful weapons."

I am Malala Yousafzai,
and I know that education helps us all *soar*.

RIGHT TO
EDUCATION!

"One child, one teacher, one pen,
and one book can change the world."
—MALALA YOUSAFZAI

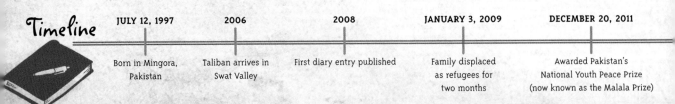

Timeline

JULY 12, 1997	2006	2008	JANUARY 3, 2009	DECEMBER 20, 2011
Born in Mingora, Pakistan	Taliban arrives in Swat Valley	First diary entry published	Family displaced as refugees for two months	Awarded Pakistan's National Youth Peace Prize (now known as the Malala Prize)

With Syrian refugees at Malala Yousafzai
All-Girls School in Lebanon, 2015

Meeting President Obama and his family
at the White House, 2013

The Yousafzai family, 2018

Speaking at the United Nations, 2013

OCTOBER 9, 2012

Shot by masked gunman

JULY 12, 2013

Addresses United Nations
Youth Assembly

DECEMBER 2014

Wins Nobel Peace Prize

2020

Graduates from Oxford
University

For Jessica Herthel,
who always picks the best fights—
especially when it's something she believes in
—B.M.

For Katie Verde,
a smart, kind, and generous young woman
who has the power to change the world for good.
—C.E.

For historical accuracy, we used Malala Yousafzai's actual words whenever possible. For more of her true voice, we recommend and acknowledge the below works. Special thanks to the amazing Malala Yousafzai, Taylor Royle, and all our friends at Malala Fund, as well as Saif Ishoof and Nick Marell for their input on early drafts.

SOURCES

I Am Malala: The Girl Who Stood Up for Education and Was Shot by the Taliban
by Malala Yousafzai with Christina Lamb (Little, Brown, 2013)

I Am Malala: How One Girl Stood Up for Education and Changed the World (Young Readers Edition)
by Malala Yousafzai and Patricia McCormick (Little, Brown, 2014)

We Are Displaced: My Journey and Stories from Refugee Girls Around the World
by Malala Yousafzai with Liz Welch (Little, Brown, 2018)

Let Her Fly: A Father's Journey by Ziauddin Yousafzai with Louise Carpenter (Little, Brown, 2018)

Class Dismissed in Swat Valley, documentary by Adam B. Ellick and Irfan Ashraf (*New York Times*, 2009)

"Diary of a Pakistani schoolgirl" (BBC News, 2009)

He Named Me Malala, documentary directed by Davis Guggenheim (Searchlight Pictures, 2015)

FURTHER READING FOR KIDS

Malala's Magic Pencil by Malala Yousafzai and Kerascoët (Little, Brown, 2017)

Muslim Girls Rise by Saira Mir and Aaliya Jaleel (Simon & Schuster, 2019)

Who Is Malala Yousafzai? by Dinah Brown (Penguin Workshop, 2015)

DIAL BOOKS FOR YOUNG READERS
An imprint of Penguin Random House LLC, New York

First published in the United States of America by Dial Books for Young Readers, an imprint of Penguin Random House LLC, 2022
Text copyright © 2022 by Forty-four Steps, Inc. • Illustrations copyright © 2022 by Christopher Eliopoulos

Dial and colophon are registered trademarks of Penguin Random House LLC.

Visit us online at penguinrandomhouse.com.

Library of Congress Cataloging-in-Publication Data is available.

Photo on page 38 by Antonio Zazueta Olmos. Page 39: photo of Malala with Syrian refugees by Wael Hamzeh/EPA/Shutterstock,
Malala at the White House by Pete Souza/The White House/Getty Images, Yousafzai family photo by Abdullah Sherin/AP/Shutterstock,
and Malala at the UN by STAN HONDA/AFP/Getty Images

ISBN 9780593405888 • Printed in the United States of America • 10 9 8 7 6 5 4 3 2 1
PC
Designed by Jason Henry • Text set in Triplex • The artwork for this book was created digitally.